MIC

GW01319622

A Ghost in Love

and Other Plays

OXFORD UNIVERSITY PRESS

1999

Oxford University Press,
Great Clarendon Street, Oxford OX2 6DP

Oxford New York

Athens Auckland Bangkok Bogotá Buenos Aires Calcutta Cape Town
Chennai Dar es Salaam Delhi Florence Hong Kong Istanbul Karachi
Kuala Lumpur Madrid Melbourne Mexico City Mumbai Nairobi
Paris São Paulo Singapore Taipei Tokyo Toronto Warsaw
and associated companies in
Berlin Ibadan

ISBN 0 19 422854 1

First published 1999

Illustrated by Kay Dixey/Linda Rogers Associates

Printed in Hong Kong

CONTENTS

INTRODUCTION

Richard Little is at home on a dark night in 1653. Two years ago, his sister Beth's husband, James, died. She found a new husband. But the man at the window in the dark night is James Heston. And he is angry with Richard . . .

CHARACTERS IN THE PLAY

Richard Little
Mary Little, Richard's wife
The ghost of James Heston, Richard's brother-in-law
David Keech, Beth's second husband
Judge Timms
Oliver Barker, who speaks for Richard in court
Philip Reynolds, who speaks against Richard in court
Six women and six men

PERFORMANCE NOTES

Scene 1: A room with a book, a table, chairs and a dress for Mary to have in her hand.
Scene 2: In court, with the judge's chair, chairs for six men and six women, something to eat, a bag, money.
Scene 3: The same room as Scene 1, with a knife, table and chairs.
Scene 4: In prison, with a bed, table, chair and book.
You will need black clothes for the men, long dresses for the women. The tables and chairs only move in Scenes 1 and 4 in the character's head; they do not move on the stage. In Scene 2 we hear Heston's ghost, but we cannot see him.

One Ghost for the Day, One Ghost for the Night

A ghost comes to Richard Little

*The year is 1653. It is a cold, dark winter night and
Richard Little, a man of forty, is sitting in his chair. He
is reading a book. He hears something. He goes to the
window, looks out and then goes back to the chair. His
wife, Mary, comes in. She is making a dress. She has the
dress in her hand.*

RICHARD Mary, I can hear something outside.

MARY There's nothing there. Read your book, Richard.

RICHARD Come and sit with me.

MARY No. I'm making a dress. I'm going upstairs.

RICHARD Mary, please. There's something out there.

MARY Oh, Richard!

  Mary goes out and James Heston's ghost comes in.

HESTON Hello, Richard.

RICHARD Aaaagh! You! James! James Heston! But you –
  you're dead!

HESTON Yes. I am dead. But I can't find peace because of
  you.

RICHARD Because of me? Why – why because of me?

'My boy gets my money at twenty-one and not before.'

HESTON Beth had a new husband after me. That animal, Keech.

RICHARD Yes. Beth was a good woman. And a good sister to me. I said to her, 'Don't go with Keech. Think of James. He's dead now.'

HESTON She was Keech's wife for only three months. Then she died. And now Keech has my son. And he has my son's money.

RICHARD Ah. I understand now.

HESTON Oh, you remember now? Before I died, I said to you, 'My boy gets my money at twenty-one and not before'. He is eight now. Eight. And Keech has his money.

RICHARD I'm sorry about that, but what can I do?

HESTON You must get my boy's money. Get it from Keech.

RICHARD No! Keech can kill me with one hand. He's big – he always has a knife in his pocket. Last year he killed a man with that knife. I'm afraid of him, James.

HESTON Are you afraid of me?

RICHARD No. Oh! Yes, a little. You're a ghost!

HESTON Only a little, eh? Look at the table.

RICHARD (*Looking at the table*) Oh no! The table is moving! (*He stands up and walks to the table.*) Oh no! Oh, the chair is moving now! And now my chair is moving! James! Don't do this to me!

HESTON At this minute, Keech is building a new home in a village near here with my son's money. Stop him!

RICHARD I'm sorry, James. I can't. (*He gets a book and throws it across the room.*) I didn't want – that was my hand but – James, can you get in my head? Can you tell my hand—
He looks at his hand and at the book.

HESTON (*Laughing*) Yes, Richard. And your answer is going to be 'Yes'. Or you are going to do this again and again and again and—
Richard gets a book and throws it across the

3

room again. Then he runs across the room. Then he moves the table, the chairs and his chair. Heston laughs. Richard stops.

RICHARD I'm going mad! Why does my hand throw a book, when I don't want to? Can all dead people do this? Can they get in a man's head, so he moves a chair or throws a book?

HESTON Oh yes. Now, I can do it to you again or you can say 'Yes' and get my son's money. Which?

RICHARD But how? How can I get the money from Keech?

HESTON Sit down. I'm going to tell you.

'I'm going mad!'

SCENE 2

David Keech in court

In the court we can see Judge Timms, Keech, Barker, Reynolds, Richard and Mary. There are six women and six men behind Keech. They are from the village and they are watching the trial. Judge Timms is in a big chair in front of the court.

BARKER (*Standing*) My name is Oliver Barker. And I speak for Richard Little here today.
He sits. Reynolds stands up.

REYNOLDS Judge Timms. I speak for David Keech here today. My name is Philip Reynolds. (*He sits.*)

WOMAN 1 That Keech took the boy's money. You can see it in his face.

WOMAN 2 Oh Lil, we must listen to Oliver Barker and Philip Reynolds first.

MAN 1 Keech is the boy Tom's father now.

MAN 2 A good father doesn't take his son's money and build a new house with it.

TIMMS Be quiet in my court!

WOMAN 1 Sorry!

TIMMS Oliver Barker. You can begin.

BARKER (*Standing*) Judge Timms. Before James Heston died, he said this to Richard Little. He said, 'My

5

boy gets my money at twenty-one and not before.'

TIMMS (*Writing*) 'At twenty-one and not before . . .'

The trial of David Keech.

BARKER   Yes, judge. But Keech has this money now. The boy's money. He is building a big house with it. We all know that.

MAN 1   (*Starting to eat something*) Put Keech in prison, I say.

MAN 6   (*Eating*) Five years.

WOMAN 6   (*Eating*) No, ten.

TIMMS   You! Don't eat in my court! Philip Reynolds. Speak.

REYNOLDS   (*Standing*) Judge Timms. Yes, there is a house in a village near here. And, yes, it is Keech's house. But the money for it is not young Tom's money.

TIMMS   (*Writing*) Not Tom's money.

REYNOLDS   No, Judge Timms. It is David Keech's money. *Reynolds sits.*

BARKER   (*Standing*) So one day Keech is not rich and the next day he *is* rich? He has money for a house? *Men and women laugh. Barker sits.*

REYNOLDS   (*Standing*) Call David Keech. *Keech stands in front of Judge Timms.*

REYNOLDS   David Keech. Where is the boy Tom's money? Do you have it at home?

KEECH   No.

WOMAN 3   Keech took the money! It was Keech!

WOMAN 6   I said, 'Keech took the money!' I said that yesterday!

KEECH   I have the money here. In this court.

MEN AND WOMEN 1–3   (*All talking*) No! Never! Keech didn't take the money then! The money's here! Here in this court!

KEECH   The money is under my chair. You! Woman! Bring me the money!

WOMAN 1   Me?

KEECH   Yes, you! (*There is a bag under Keech's chair. Woman 1 takes it and gives it to Keech.*)

WOMAN 1   Here you are. (*She sits down again.*)

KEECH   (*Opening the bag and taking out money*) Here! Judge Timms! Here! Richard Little! Here! Look, everybody! Here is the money! So I didn't take it from the boy! You hear me, Richard Little?

RICHARD   (*Afraid*) Yes.

TIMMS   One minute! Richard Little.

RICHARD   (*Standing, looking afraid*) Yes, Judge Timms?

TIMMS   You said, 'Keech took the boy's money'. You said that. Why? Why, man, why? Why say that?

RICHARD   Because – because. Because James Heston came to my home. James Heston said it to me.

MEN AND WOMEN 4–6   (*All talking*) James Heston? Did he say 'Heston'? Heston's dead. A ghost came?

TIMMS   Richard Little, James Heston is dead. He died in 1651.

MEN AND WOMEN   (*All laughing and talking*) He talked to a

dead man! James Heston! Oh, that's a laugh!

MARY (*Standing*) Judge Timms. My husband is ill. In our house he talks to people and there is nobody there. Can I take him home now, please?

The men and women are all laughing.

RICHARD I am not ill! Stop laughing! Be quiet, all of you! Sit down, Mary.

Men and women stop laughing. Mary sits down.

RICHARD Thank you! (*It is quiet in the court now.*) Yes, James Heston is dead. And yes, James Heston spoke to me. I want James Heston here. Now. He can tell you.

'Can I take him home now, please?'

9

MAN 4   He *is* ill!

MAN 5   He's mad!

WOMAN 4   Let's listen to him.

WOMAN 5   Yes, we can listen to him.

TIMMS   Be quiet! Call James Heston! I say, call James
Heston to this court!

KEECH   Heston is dead, man! And Richard Little is mad!

TIMMS   Call James Heston!

*For a minute, we can hear nothing. Then we hear
James Heston's voice, but we cannot see him.*

HESTON'S GHOST   I am James Heston.

MEN AND WOMEN   Aaaaaagh! Oh! Oh, but he's dead!

KEECH   No! No! Oh please no!

MEN AND WOMEN   (*All talking*) It's Heston! Is Heston dead,
then? Aaaagh! Oh I'm afraid! Oh please!

TIMMS   James Heston? Is it you? Did you speak to
Richard Little?

HESTON'S GHOST   Yes.

TIMMS   What did you say?

HESTON'S GHOST   I told him, Keech took my boy's money.
And then Keech killed a man in the next village.
He was a rich man. Keech took his money. You
see the money now. Here. In this court.

KEECH   Aaagh! I can't kill Heston. Heston is dead. But
you! You, Richard Little! You brought me to this
court. I'm going to kill you next!

10

Keech runs out of the court.

TIMMS Stop him! Stop him!

MEN AND WOMEN (*All talking*) It was Keech! Keech took
the money! I said that! I said, 'Keech took the
money!'

TIMMS This court says, 'Keech took the money. And
Keech killed a man.' Now find David Keech and
bring him to me!

SCENE 3

Keech finds Richard Little

Richard is sitting in his chair, at home.

RICHARD What's that? Can I hear something? Mary, is
that you? Oh no, it's not James again! James, is
that you? (*He looks at the door, very afraid.*)
Aaaagh! Oh no!

David Keech comes in. He has a knife.

RICHARD Oh no! Keech, please! No!

*Keech kills Richard, then runs away. Mary
comes in and sees Richard.*

MARY Oh no! Not Richard. Not my darling, darling
Richard. Keech killed him. You're going to go to
prison for this, Keech.

SCENE 4

A visit for Keech in prison

*Keech is in prison. He is sitting on his bed. He has a
table, a chair and a book there, too.*

KEECH   Hello? What's that? Is there someone there?
         Aaagh! My table! My table is moving. (*He
         stands.*) Aaagh! Now the bed's moving. Am I ill?
         Oh my head! (*He puts his head in his hands.*)
         Oh! Now the chair is moving. What's
         happening? (*He takes the book and throws it
         across the room.*) Why did I do that? Am I mad?
         It was my hand but—
         The ghost of Richard comes in.

KEECH   Aaaaghh! You're dead! I killed you!

RICHARD Yes. I'm dead. And you killed me. But I'm not
         going away. I'm staying here, in prison with you.
         *Keech wants to hit Richard's ghost, but he
         cannot. Richard laughs.*

RICHARD You can't hit me now. You can't hit a ghost.
         And you can't kill me again. But we can talk. We
         have time for that. We have all day.
         Keech throws a book across the room.

RICHARD And you can do that all day too.

KEECH   All day? All the time?

12

RICHARD Yes. (*He lies on the bed.*) Now throw the book across the room again. (*Keech does it.*) And again and again and again.

KEECH (*Throwing the book again and again*) Oh no! Please! Are all my days going to be like this?

RICHARD Your days, yes. And for your nights – I have a friend here.

(*James Heston's ghost comes in.*)

HESTON Hello, Richard. Hello, David.

KEECH You! You here too!

HESTON (*Smiling*) Yes. David, throw the book across the room, please. (*Keech does it.*) Thank you. I'm going to be here at night, David. And you have Richard here every day. All right?

KEECH Oh no! No!

HESTON One ghost for the day, one ghost for the night. Now throw the book across the room again.

Keech does it. Richard and Heston laugh.

13

INTRODUCTION

Jenny Lawson was an actress and her husband Gilbert is a film director. Now Jenny stays at home, in their nice house, but she wants more. She wants to live a little before she dies! Gilbert loves Jenny, but a wife must stay at home, he thinks. Suddenly something happens to Gilbert, and then he understands Jenny. But is it too late?

CHARACTERS IN THE PLAY

Jenny Lawson, a film actress
Gilbert Lawson, Jenny's husband, a film director
Henry, a young man, a film student
Laura, a friend of Jenny's from school
Jenny's father
Jenny's mother
A waitress at the airport café
Two women and one man at the airport
British Airways man at the airport check-in desk

PERFORMANCE NOTES

Scene 1: In a garden with a table, two chairs, breakfast (with bread), a book.
Scene 2: At the airport café, with a table, two chairs, a big bag, a coffee, a coke, a sandwich.
Scene 3: A check-in desk, some plane tickets.
Scene 4: A room with a table, three chairs, a telephone.
Jenny must have a watch.

Sleep now, My Darling

Jenny must stay at home

It is a hot summer day. Jenny and Gilbert Lawson are having breakfast at a table in their garden. Gilbert is reading a book.

JENNY   Gilbert, can I come with you? To America?

GILBERT   (*He is reading. Looking up*) What?

JENNY   Oh, Gilbert! Please listen to me! I said 'Can I come to America too?'

GILBERT   (*Eating some bread*) Mmmm. This is good bread. Did you make it?

JENNY   Yes. Gilbert! I said, 'Can I come with you?'

GILBERT   No, Jenny. You have work here. There's the house, the garden . . .
He begins to read his book again.

JENNY   I remember *My New Friend*. It was your best film. It was my best film, too! They were happy days.

GILBERT   (*He puts the book down, smiling.*) Yes. I watched *My New Friend* again last week. It's the best Gilbert Lawson film. And you were good in it, my love! You're a good actress.

15

JENNY   (*Smiling*) The film had a good director! Gilbert Lawson!

GILBERT   Oh, thank you! But now I have this new film, so I must go to America for six weeks.

JENNY   Gilbert, can I be in this film, too? I want to be an actress again.

GILBERT   Perhaps next time. Would you like that? Perhaps you can be in the next film.

JENNY   You said that before.

GILBERT   Did I? (*Eating again*) Yes, this bread is very good.

JENNY   Can we go to America together then? Not for a film. Just you and me. Perhaps next year?

GILBERT   Perhaps. (*He smiles at her.*)

JENNY   (*Smiling at him*) Next year, then.

GILBERT   Yes. Next year. Love, I must go now. I'm going

'*Yes, this bread is very good.*'

16

to be late for the plane. I love you, Jenny.

JENNY   (*Unhappily*) I love you, too, darling.

SCENE 2

Jenny talks to a film student

It is six weeks later. Jenny is having a coffee at the airport. She is waiting for Gilbert's plane. A young man, Henry, sees her. Henry has a big bag in his hand.

HENRY   Hello! Are you Jenny Lawson?

JENNY   Yes.

HENRY   I knew it!

    A young waitress brings Jenny's coffee. She smiles at Henry.

WAITRESS   (*To Jenny*) Here you are. (*To Henry*) And do you want something?

JENNY   (*To the waitress*) Thanks. (*To Henry*) Sorry, but do I know you?

HENRY   (*To the waitress*) A coke for me please, and a sandwich.

WAITRESS   (*She smiles at Henry.*) One coke, one sandwich. (*She goes away.*)

HENRY   (*To Jenny*) Oh sorry – yes. I know your film, *My New Friend*. And I know Gilbert. Can I sit down?

JENNY   (*Smiling*) You can't stand up and have a coke

and a sandwich. Wait a minute. I know you. I know your face. But I can't remember – tell me, how do you know Gilbert?

Henry sits down at the table with Jenny.

HENRY I'm learning about his work. I know all the Gilbert Lawson films. But forget about me. I want to talk about you. You aren't happy. I can see that.

JENNY (*Angrily*) What? You can't say that!

The waitress comes back with a coke and a sandwich.

WAITRESS (*She puts the things down and smiles at Henry.*) A coke and a sandwich.

HENRY Thank you.

WAITRESS That's OK. The sandwiches are very good. I have them for lunch sometimes.

HENRY (*Smiling and eating the sandwich*) Yes, you're right. It's very good. Thank you.

WAITRESS That's OK. Goodbye then. (*She goes.*)

JENNY (*Looking at her watch*) I must go soon.

HENRY What do you do every day?

JENNY What? I don't know you. You can't ask—

HENRY (*Smiling*) Jenny. Please. Tell me. What do you do every day?

Jenny begins to cry. Henry smiles, but nicely.

JENNY (*Crying, angry*) OK. Here's your answer. I get up in the morning and then I do nothing. We have no

'I was happy when I was an actress.'

children. A woman does the house for me. A man
does the garden.

HENRY Do you have friends?

JENNY (*Crying*) Yes! No! I have coffee with people. I
have dinner with people. We say things like, 'Nice
weather for the time of year'. But we don't talk.

HENRY Yes. I understand. Now I'm going to tell you
about me. I'm twenty. I go to America,
sometimes. I have friends. I like films, so I make
films. I'm happy. What about you?

JENNY (*She stops crying.*) I was happy when I was an
actress.

HENRY There! There's your answer! Be an actress again.
Laura comes in. She sees Jenny.

LAURA Jenny Lawson!

JENNY Laura!

LAURA What are you doing here?

JENNY   Waiting for Gilbert.

LAURA   (*Smiling at Henry*) And who is this?

HENRY   My name is Henry. I'm a film student.

JENNY   Sit down, Laura, please.

LAURA   No. I can't stop. My children are here. We are all going to America. All the family. I write books now, you know. What do you do?

JENNY   Me? Nothing.

LAURA   Have you got children?

JENNY   No.

LAURA   You look unhappy, Jenny. At school you were beautiful and good at everything. And now you are older, with no work and no children. Oh dear!

JENNY   What? Laura! Why did you say that?
Laura goes. Jenny is very unhappy.

HENRY   I have to go now. (*He picks up his bag.*)

JENNY   What's – what's that name on your bag? (*Reading the name*) Henry Gilbert Lawson. I know you now! Gilbert! You are Gilbert, when he was twenty years old. But – why are you here? Oh no! Aaaaggghhh!
Henry runs out.

20

SCENE 3
Jenny learns about Gilbert

There are four people at the check-in, Woman 1, Woman 2, a man and Jenny's father. They are waiting. A British Airways man is looking at Father's plane ticket. Jenny runs in.

JENNY Excuse me! Oh, father! What are you doing here?

FATHER Jenny, smile. Be happy.

JENNY What?

WOMAN 1 (*To Jenny*) Hey! I was here before you.

MAN (*To Jenny*) I was in front of you, too.

WOMAN 2 (*To Jenny*) Are you OK, love? (*To Woman 1 and man*) She's white in the face!

JENNY (*To the British Airways man*) Excuse me . . .

BRITISH AIRWAYS MAN (*Looking at tickets*) Can you wait, please?

JENNY No! My name is Jenny Lawson . . .

BRITISH AIRWAYS MAN Ah! Mrs Lawson! We phoned you at home. There was no answer. Mrs Lawson, I'm sorry, but Mr Lawson's plane crashed in the sea. He's dead.

JENNY Oh no!!!

SCENE 4
Jenny understands everything

Jenny's father and mother and Jenny are all sitting at a table.

JENNY They all died. All the people on the plane.
MOTHER Oh Jenny!
FATHER Your mother and I are so sorry, my love.
JENNY Thank you. Why were you at the airport, father?
FATHER Me? I wasn't at the airport.
JENNY Yes, you were! You were at the British Airways

'Your mother and I are so sorry.'

check-in desk. You said
'Be happy.' Then you left.

FATHER No!

JENNY Wait a minute.
(*Telephoning*) Hello,
Laura? Laura, this is
Jenny Lawson. We were
at school together. Laura,
I saw you at the airport,
remember, and – oh!

MOTHER What is Laura saying?

JENNY She said, 'I wasn't at the
airport.' (*Into the
telephone*) Laura, one
question. Do you write books now? Yes. Thank
you. (*Putting the phone down, and speaking to
her father and mother*) She writes books.

MOTHER Is that important?

JENNY Yes. Laura wants to write books, so she writes
books. And she's happy. At the airport, father
said 'Be happy.' And Henry Gilbert Lawson said
'Be an actress again.'

MOTHER I understand.

JENNY I understand now, too. My darling husband, I'm
going to be an actress for you, again. A good
actress. Thank you. So sleep now, my darling.

*'Laura, this is
Jenny Lawson.'*

INTRODUCTION

Brad and Jerry are nineteen, and they are in Britain on holiday. It is an unhappy time for Brad: his father died last month. His father was Dick Davis of Davis TV and when he goes back to America, Brad is going to be Brad Davis of Davis TV. One hot day, Brad and Jerry stop at a hotel in a village, and some strange things happen there . . .

CHARACTERS IN THE PLAY

Brad Davis, a young American man, aged nineteen
Jerry Maloney, Brad's friend
The ghost of Ellen Bannister
Mrs Finch, from the hotel
Maud Anscombe, an old woman from the village
Mrs Morgan, who works in the village shop
Three women and two men from the village

PERFORMANCE NOTES

Scene 1: A hotel room with two bags, a book about Britain, a television, a bed, a watch for Brad.
Scene 2: A room with a table and three chairs.
Scene 3: In a shop, with two cokes, sandwiches, money.
Scenes 4 and 5: The same room as Scene 1, with a bed and a television.
Scene 6: In the street, with two bags.
You will need summer shirts for Brad and Jerry, and a long dress for Ellen. The television doesn't have to work.

A Ghost in Love

Brad sees a ghost

Brad and Jerry come into the hotel room and put their
bags down. It is a hot day and they are wearing summer
shirts. Brad sits on a bed.

JERRY   Man, I want a drink. Twenty miles in one
morning! Are the bicycles OK, in the street ?

BRAD   In this little village? Oh yes! Nobody steals
bicycles here.

JERRY   How do you know? This is your first time here.
First time in England. Or am I wrong?

BRAD   No, you're right. But – I remember this village. I
was here before, Jerry. I can feel it.

JERRY   Oh come on! We were out in the sun for five
hours. You need to drink some cold water, my
friend!

BRAD   This hotel opened in 1853, right?

JERRY   (*He gets a book about Britain out of his bag and*
looks in it.) Right. Brad, you looked at this book
before.

BRAD   No, I didn't. Hey, you know something? (*He looks*
at his watch.) It's one-fifteen. My dad died at this

25

minute, on this day last month.

JERRY   Oh, Brad. I'm sorry.

BRAD   No, no. It's OK. I'm going to go back to New
York next week, after our three weeks in
England. And I'm going to be 'Brad Davis, of
Davis TV'. Dad wanted that.

They stayed at the hotel in the village.

26

JERRY   Yeah. Hey, come on! Let's go out in the sun. Let's see the village. Have a drink. Find some girls.

BRAD   No, you go. I like it here. Here in the room.

JERRY   OK. Let's stay in the room. Hey! There's a television. (*Jerry puts the television on but nothing happens.*) Hmm.

BRAD   Not working? Oh, forget it.

JERRY   No! You're Brad Davis of Davis Television, the biggest in America. You must have a television! Look, shall I go down and ask Mrs Finch? You stay here. You look tired.

BRAD   Yeah, thanks, Jerry. I am tired.
Jerry goes out. Brad looks at the book about Britain.

BRAD   (*Reading from the book*) 'In 1760 the hotel was a house. A family called Bannister lived in the house. One day, the nineteen-year-old daughter, Ellen—'
The ghost of Ellen Bannister comes in. She is wearing a dress from 1760.

ELLEN   I was never nineteen. I died at eighteen.

BRAD   Yes, I remember you. Hello, Ellen.

ELLEN   Hello, Matthew. Why does your friend call you Brad? Is that a name?

BRAD   Yes. It's an American name.

ELLEN   But you are Matthew and I'm going to call you Matthew. Always. Oh Matthew. I waited and

waited and waited for you. I love you so much.
Do you love me?

BRAD   Yes. I think – Yes, I do.

'Hello, Ellen.'

ELLEN   You think! Is that an answer? After all these
         years? Oh Matthew! Matthew, do you remember
         everything?

BRAD   No, not everything. I remember our love. And
         you died, I remember that. I wanted to die too.
         And again last month, I wanted to die.

ELLEN   Oh Matthew! Don't say that! Oh Matthew, I'm
         so happy to see you again.

BRAD   Ellen. Can I see you? Can we talk?

ELLEN   Oh yes. I want to talk to you about—
         Jerry comes in with Mrs Finch. Ellen runs out.

MRS FINCH   Are you OK, love? You look white.

JERRY   This is not a happy time for Brad.

MRS FINCH   I'm sorry, love. Do you want some dinner? I
         make the best dinner in the north of England.

'I make the best dinner in the north of England.'

BRAD   (*Smiling*) No, thank you.

MRS FINCH Talk to me later, then. Right, the television.
(*She hits the television.*) It's OK now. Bye-bye,
Brad. Bye, Jerry. Have a nice time in our village.
She goes to the door.

BRAD   Mrs Finch! Wait, please. Do you know about the
Bannister family?

MRS FINCH Did you see the ghost? Ellen Bannister?

BRAD   Yes.

JERRY   What? Brad, you saw a ghost? Oh, come on!

MRS FINCH Oh, Ellen's always here. She likes young men.
She's always looking for her boyfriend.
Matthew's his name, I think.

BRAD   Mrs Finch, what happened? How did she die?
What happened to Matthew?

MRS FINCH You're interested, love, I can see that. There's
an old woman in the village. Her name is Maud
Anscombe. She knows about Ellen. You ask
Maud. (*She goes out.*)

JERRY   Brad, this ghost – What did she say?

BRAD   (*Not looking at Jerry*) She – she didn't speak,
Jerry. She said nothing at all.

SCENE 2

Brad and Jerry want to know about Ellen

Maud is a very old woman. Her hair is white. Brad and Jerry are sitting at a table with her in her house.

MAUD   Ellen Bannister? A bad, bad girl. When she looked at someone, the next day they were ill.

JERRY   So she was a witch?

MAUD   Yes. She looked at animals too. Then all the cows in the village had no milk in them.

BRAD   (*Angrily*) Do – do you know this? How do you know? How can you know?

MAUD   Oh, it's in all the books. Our village is famous because of bad Ellen Bannister.

'Then all the cows in the village had no milk in them.'

31

SCENE 3

Was Ellen a witch?

Brad and Jerry are in Mrs Morgan's village shop. There are two men and three women in the shop, and Mrs Morgan.

MRS MORGAN   Yes? Are you next?

JERRY   Yes. Two cokes please. And two of those sandwiches.

BRAD   I'm not hungry.

JERRY   Man, you must eat. You can't sit in your room all day and wait for a ghost.

Mrs Morgan gets the cokes and the sandwiches.

MRS MORGAN   That's six pounds, please. (*Jerry gives her the money.*) What ghost's this? Ellen Bannister?

BRAD   (*Angrily*) Yes!

JERRY   Do you know about Ellen Bannister?

MRS MORGAN   Oh, people in our village had no money then. Of course they stole things. And Ellen Bannister sold them. She only wanted to help.

JERRY   Was she a witch? Some people say that.

MRS MORGAN   A witch? (*Laughing*) No, of course not. The men loved her. She helped them, you see. The women didn't love her so much. She was beautiful, you see.

'He stole things from rich people.'

WOMAN 1 Her boyfriend was the bad one, that Matthew.
It wasn't her.

BRAD (*Drinking his coke*) Oh. What did he do?

WOMAN 2 He stole things from rich people. Then she sold
them and he took all the money. He took all her
money, too. But she loved him.

BRAD Did he love her?

MAN 1 No. He had two or three women.

WOMAN 3 No, he didn't! He loved her. He lived for her.

MAN 2 Who are you talking about? That witch Ellen
Bannister? She ate cats for breakfast.

WOMAN 3 (*To Brad and Jerry*) Oh, don't listen to him.

MRS MORGAN (*Laughing*) Don't listen to these people, you
boys. What happened to Ellen Bannister? You
want to know that? Matthew killed her.

Scene 4

Where is Ellen now?

It is night time. Jerry is sitting on the bed. Brad is walking up and down.

BRAD   Seven hours. We waited seven hours. Where is she, Jerry?

JERRY   I said this before. I don't know. Just wait.

BRAD   She isn't coming, because you're here.

JERRY   Brad, I say again. One. I sleep here. This is my room. Two. I am your friend and I am not leaving you like this.

BRAD   Jerry, is this all a big laugh for you?

JERRY   No. Not now. I want to see Ellen, too. I want to help.

BRAD   OK. Thanks, Jerry. Sorry. Hey, here she is.
The ghost of Ellen comes into the room.

BRAD   Ellen, Ellen. It's me, Brad, Matthew.

JERRY   Man, oh man! It's all true!

BRAD   Ellen, please. Tell me, what happened, in 1760?

ELLEN   You must remember!

BRAD   No.

ELLEN   We sold things, you and me. Rich people's things. You stole them, remember?

JERRY   Wow! Brad, you were Robin Hood! Sorry!

34

ELLEN   The rich people didn't like me. They said bad
        things about me. 'Ellen Bannister is a witch.'
        They said that, but it's not true.

BRAD   Of course not.

ELLEN   Then, one day, they came for us. Twenty men.

BRAD   What happened?

ELLEN   We ran away. You found a ship. A ship going to
        America. You said, 'See you at one-fifteen. At the
        harbour. We can go away, you and me.'

BRAD   And then what happened, Ellen?

ELLEN   The ship went early. I wasn't there in time. You
        went on the ship. You didn't wait for me.

BRAD   Oh no!

'You didn't wait for me.'

ELLEN   When I arrived, there were a lot of ships there. I
         didn't know the name of our ship. I looked for
         you. I waited and waited and waited.

BRAD   Ellen! Oh Ellen, I'm sorry.

ELLEN   Then the men came. They put me in prison. I died
         three months later. And then I came back home.
         Here. And I waited again. I waited for you.

BRAD   I love you, Ellen.

ELLEN   I love you too, Matthew.

SCENE 5
What is Brad going to do?

*It is dark. Brad is standing at the window of the room.
Jerry comes in. Brad always has his back to Jerry in this
scene.*

JERRY   Do you want to die? Do you want to go to Ellen?

BRAD   Before today, the answer was 'Yes'. Matthew
         wanted to die and go to be with Ellen. Do you
         understand that?

JERRY   Yes.

BRAD   But Matthew is dead and I am Brad now.

JERRY   And what does Brad want?

BRAD   I don't know. I'm thinking. Is there a train from
         here to London tomorrow?

JERRY   Yes. We can put our bicycles on the train. We can get the next plane back to America. Do you want to do that?

BRAD   I don't know. I'm going to tell you tomorrow.

Scene 6

In love with a ghost

The next day. Brad and Jerry are in the street. Jerry has two bags. Mrs Finch is there too.

MRS FINCH You must leave, then? A week early?

JERRY Yes. I'm sorry.

Mrs Morgan comes past the hotel.

MRS MORGAN Oh hello. It's the American boys. Are you going home to America?

BRAD Jerry's going home, Mrs Morgan. I'm staying here, at the hotel. I'm going to live here. Always.

JERRY Brad, do you want to do this? Think about Davis TV. What are you going to do, here in England?

BRAD I don't know. But, yes, Davis TV needs a good man. My dad worked for years for Davis TV. But now it has a good man, Jerry. You.

JERRY Me? Oh! Thank you, Brad.

BRAD That's OK. I'm happy. I'm in love. She waited for me and now I'm here. I'm never going to leave her again.

EXERCISES

A Checking your understanding

One Ghost for the Day, One Ghost for the Night

1 *Who said these words, and to whom?*
1 'Come and sit with me.'
2 'I can't find peace because of you.'
3 'Here is the money!'
4 'Now find Keech and bring him to me!'

2 *Are these sentences about the play true (T) or false (F)?*
1 Mary saw the ghost of James Heston in her house.
2 Richard Little was mad.
3 Keech killed one man only.

Sleep now, My Darling

1 *Who said these words, and to whom?*
1 'They were happy days.'
2 'We don't talk.'
3 'Be an actress again.'
4 'Now you are older, with no work and no children.'

2 *Are these sentences about the play true (T) or false (F)?*
1 Jenny was happy at home.
2 Gilbert didn't love Jenny.
3 Henry was the ghost of Jenny's father.

A Ghost in Love

1 *Who said these words, and to whom?*
1 'You need to drink some cold water, my friend!'
2 'I was here before.'
3 'I make the best dinner in the north of England.'
4 'Then all the cows in the village had no milk in them.'

2 *Write answers to these questions.*
　1　Why did some people think that Ellen was a witch?
　2　Why did Jerry say, 'Wow! Brad, you were Robin Hood!'?
　3　Why didn't Brad go back to America?

B Working with language

One Ghost for the Day, One Ghost for the Night

1　*Put together these beginnings and endings of sentences.*
　1　she was Keech's wife
　2　go to prison for this, Keech.
　3　Keech took the money.
　4　now throw the book
　5　this court says,
　6　across the room again.
　7　you're going to
　8　for only three months.

2　*Complete these sentences with information from* **Sleep now, My Darling** *and* **A Ghost in Love**.
　1　Gilbert went to America because . . .
　2　Jenny was happy when . . .
　3　When Gilbert's plane crashed, all the people . . .
　4　Jenny meets eight people at the airport, but three of them . . .
　5　When Brad and Jerry first arrived at the hotel they felt . . .
　6　Brad was unhappy when he looked at his watch because . . .
　7　Brad remembered Ellen but he didn't remember . . .
　8　Three months after Ellen went to prison, . . .

C Activities

1 You are one of the women or men in court at the trial of David Keech. Write a letter to a friend, telling him or her what happened.

2 Gilbert wrote a short letter to Jenny before his plane crashed. Write the letter.

3 You are Jerry Maloney. It is your last evening on holiday in Britain. Write a postcard home to a friend in America.

D Project work

1 Do you know anybody who has seen a ghost? If you do, find out exactly what they saw or heard.

2 Have you read any ghost stories or seen any films about ghosts? Write down what you read or saw, or write your own ghost story.

GLOSSARY

actress a girl or woman who acts in plays or films

brother-in-law your sister's husband

build to make something (e.g. a house) by putting parts of it (e.g. wood, bricks) together

café a snack-bar or small restaurant where you can buy drinks and snacks to eat

check-in desk the place at the airport where you show your ticket and hand over your luggage

clothes things that you wear to cover your body

court a place where judges and lawyers listen to trials

cow a farm animal that gives us milk

crash (of a plane) to hit the ground and be badly damaged

darling a way of speaking to someone we love

director the person who tells actors and actresses how to act their parts or say their words

film a moving picture that you see at the cinema or on television

ghost the spirit of a dead person that comes back to visit living people

harbour a safe place for ships, while they prepare to go to sea

judge the person in a law court who decides how someone will be punished

mad of someone who is ill in the head

peace a quiet, happy time; many people hope to find peace after they die

prison a place where bad people are locked up

put on (the television) to switch on or turn on, to make it work

sell (past tense **sold**) to give something to someone who pays you for it

steal (past tense **stole**) to take things that do not belong to you

throw to lift something up and send it quickly through the air

trial a court case, to find out if someone is guilty of a crime or not

unhappy sad, not happy

voice the sound that you make when you speak

waitress a girl or woman who brings food and drinks to your table in a restaurant or café

witch a woman who uses magic to do bad things